World of Whales

Blue Whales

by Eliza Leahy

Bullfrog Books

Ideas for Parents and Teachers

Bullfrog Books let children practice reading informational text at the earliest reading levels. Repetition, familiar words, and photo labels support early readers.

Before Reading

- Discuss the cover photo. What does it tell them?
- Look at the picture glossary together. Read and discuss the words.

Read the Book

- "Walk" through the book and look at the photos. Let the child ask questions. Point out the photo labels.
- Read the book to the child, or have him or her read independently.

After Reading

- Prompt the child to think more. Ask: Blue whales are bigger than any other animal on Earth. What other big animals can you name?

Bullfrog Books are published by Jump!
5357 Penn Avenue South
Minneapolis, MN 55419
www.jumplibrary.com

Copyright © 2024 Jump! International copyright reserved in all countries. No part of this book may be reproduced in any form without written permission from the publisher.

Library of Congress Cataloging-in-Publication Data

Names: Leahy, Eliza, author.
Title: Blue whales / by Eliza Leahy.
Description: Minneapolis, MN: Jump!, Inc., [2024]
Series: World of whales | Includes index.
Audience: Ages 5–8
Identifiers: LCCN 2022051263 (print)
LCCN 2022051264 (ebook)
ISBN 9798885245890 (hardcover)
ISBN 9798885245906 (paperback)
ISBN 9798885245913 (ebook)
Subjects: LCSH: Blue whale—Juvenile literature.
Classification: LCC QL737.C424 L434 2024 (print)
LCC QL737.C424 (ebook)
DDC 599.5/248—dc23/eng/20221021
LC record available at https://lccn.loc.gov/2022051263
LC ebook record available at https://lccn.loc.gov/2022051264

Editor: Katie Chanez
Designer: Emma Almgren-Bersie

Photo Credits: Nature Picture Library/Alamy, cover, 8–9, 14–15, 23br; eco2drew/iStock, 1; Anna Che/Dreamstime, 3; WaterFrame/Alamy, 4; Chase Dekker/Shutterstock, 5; Andrea Izzotti/Shutterstock, 6–7; Mcasabar/Dreamstime, 10, 23tm; Gerald Corsi/iStock, 11, 23bm; Richard Herrmann/Minden Pictures/SuperStock, 12–13; I. Noyan Yilmaz/Shutterstock, 13, 23bl; bekirevren/Shutterstock, 14, 23tl; Hiroya Minakuchi/Minden Pictures/SuperStock, 16–17; Izanbar/Dreamstime, 18; Gohier/Visual & Written/SuperStock, 19, 23tr; Norbert Wu/Minden Pictures/SuperStock, 20–21; max-Photography/Shutterstock, 24.

Printed in the United States of America at Corporate Graphics in North Mankato, Minnesota.

Table of Contents

Big and Blue	4
Parts of a Blue Whale	22
Picture Glossary	23
Index	24
To Learn More	24

Big and Blue

What is that big swimmer?
It is a blue whale.

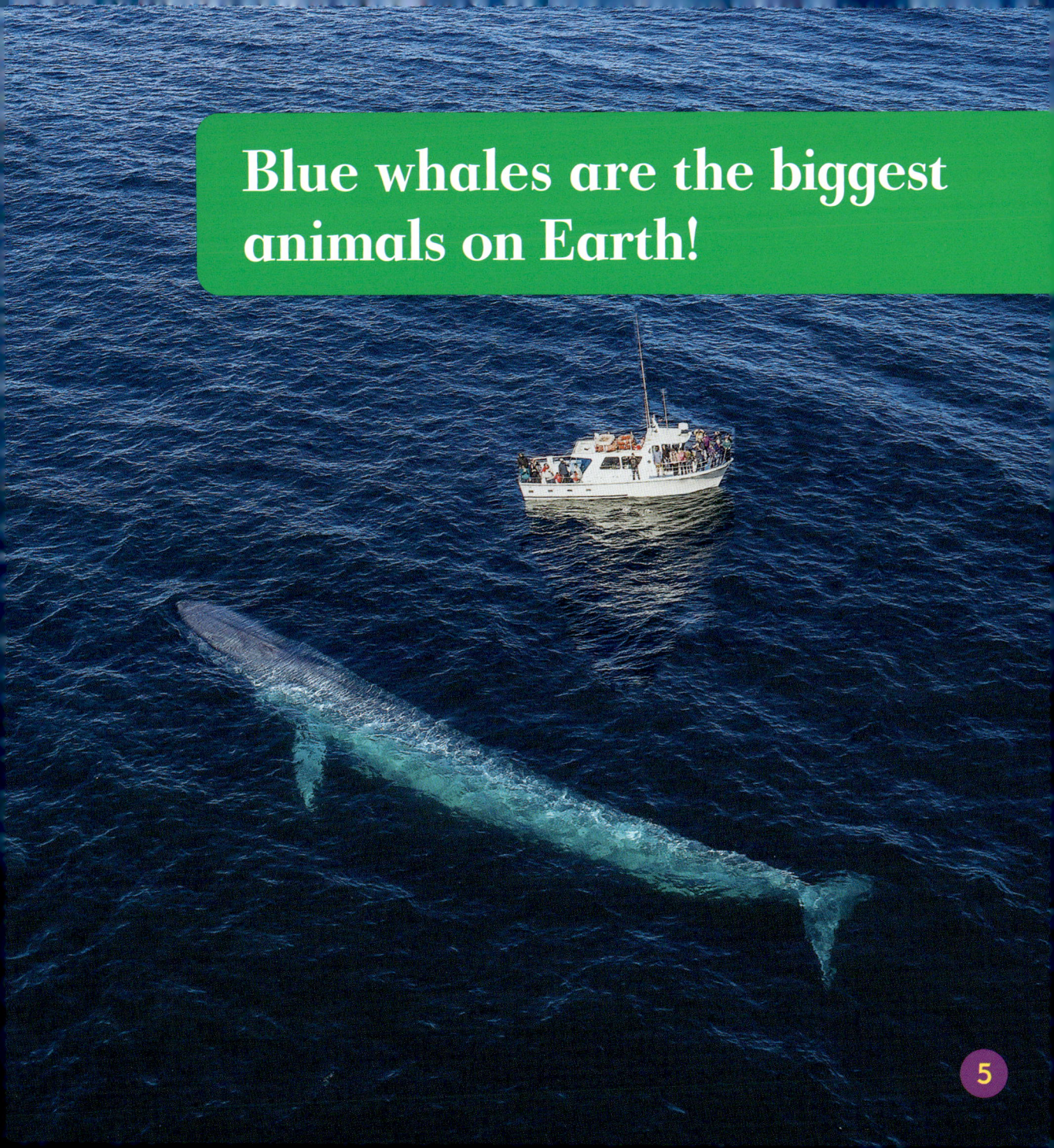

Blue whales are the biggest animals on Earth!

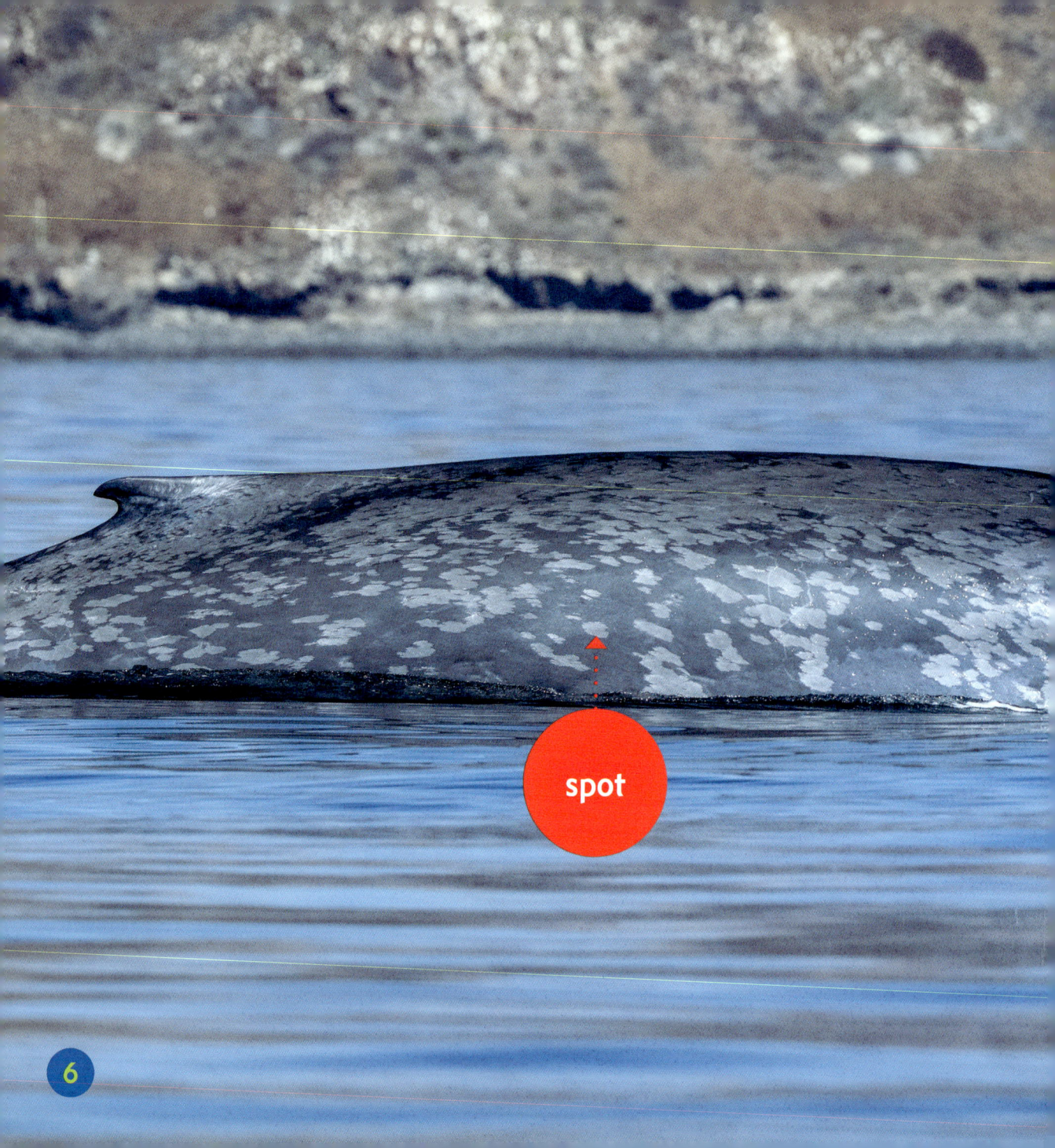

They are named for their blue color. Some also have gray spots.

Blue whales swim in all oceans. They use their fins. Tails help, too.

fin

blowholes

They breathe air.

How?

They use their blowholes.

They let air out in spouts.

spout

A blue whale dives.
Why?
It spots krill.
It hunts.

krill

Open wide!
Baleen strain water out.
Krill stay in.

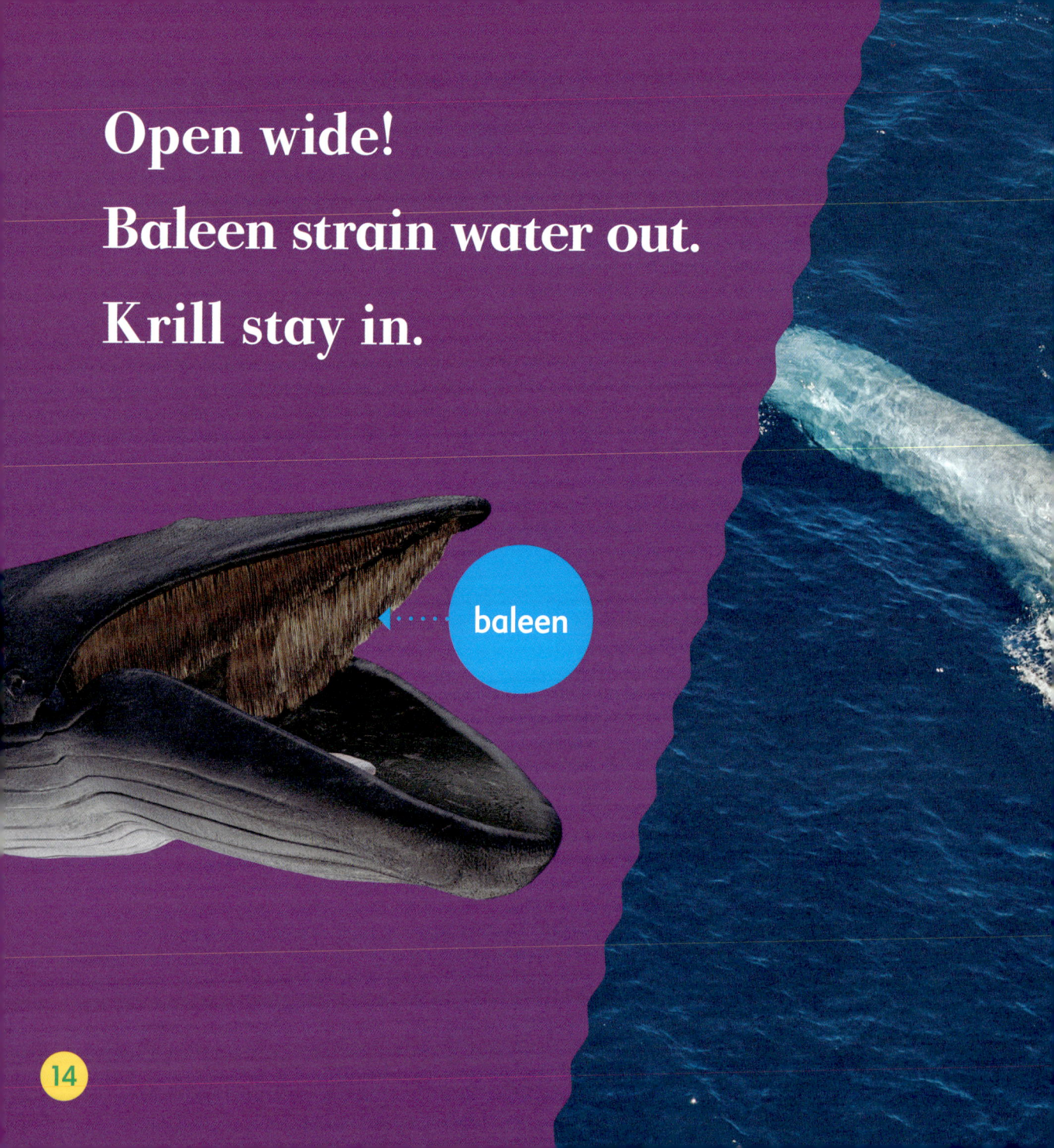

baleen

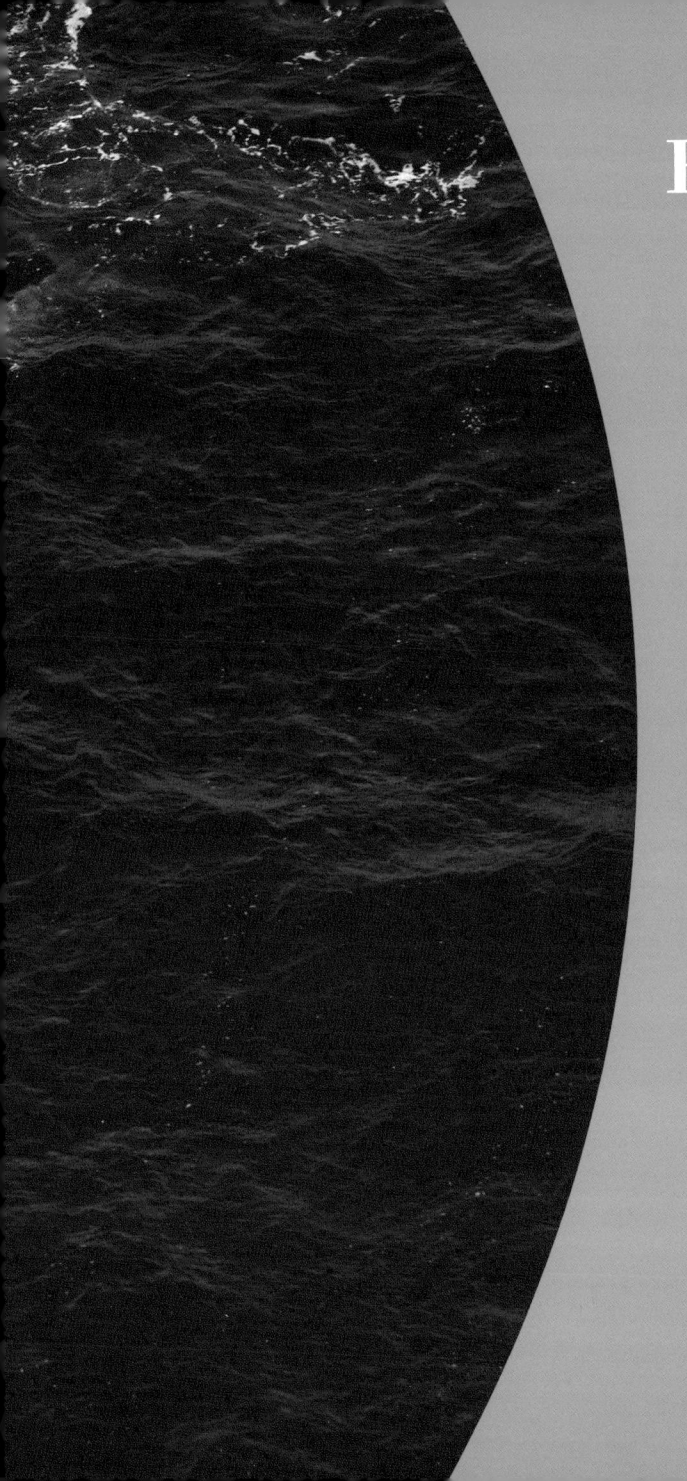

Blue whales call to each other.

They are loud.

They swim to warm water. Why?

Calves are born there.

Would you like to see a blue whale?

Parts of a Blue Whale

Blue whales can be up to 110 feet (34 meters) long. That is longer than three school buses! Take a look at the parts of a blue whale.

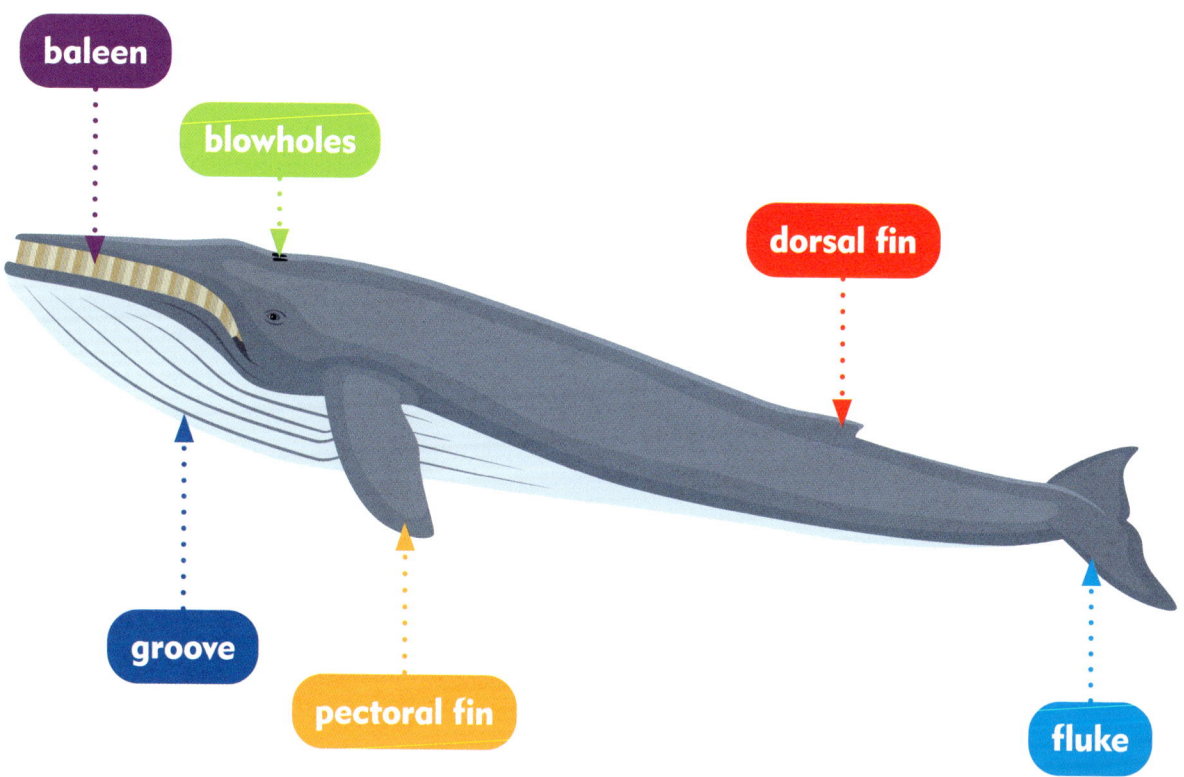

Picture Glossary

baleen
Plates in a whale's mouth that filter water and food.

blowholes
Nostrils on top of whale and dolphin heads used for breathing.

calves
Young whales.

krill
Small crustaceans that live in the ocean.

spouts
Streams of water and air that whales let out through their blowholes.

strain
To separate solids out of liquids.

Index

baleen 14
blowholes 10
calves 19
color 7
dives 13
fins 9
hunts 13
krill 13, 14
oceans 9
spouts 11
swim 9, 18
tails 9

To Learn More

Finding more information is as easy as 1, 2, 3.

❶ Go to www.factsurfer.com

❷ Enter "bluewhales" into the search box.

❸ Choose your book to see a list of websites.